The Biography
of

Saint Samaan
the Shoemaker
"the Tanner"

The Church of Saint Samaan
the Tanner
Mokattam Mountain, Cairo, Egypt.

In the name of the Father, the Son, and the Holy Spirit; one God. Amen.

The title: *The Biography of Saint Samaan the Shoemaker "the Tanner".*

The author and the publisher:
The church of Saint Samaan the Tanner in Mokattam, Cairo, Egypt.

The first english edition : *January 1994.*

The second english edition: *November 1998.*

Printed by: *MD Graphics   Tel : 5117861*

I.S.B.N   : 977 - 5529 - 01 - 8

Legal Depsit No: 3036 / 1994

For orders: *The bookstore of Saint Samaan Church in Mokattam.*

Tel. *202 512 3666 / 202 512 4080.*

FAX. *202 512 6150.*

H.H. POPE SHENOUDA III,

*117 th Pope and Patriarch of Alexandria
and the See of St. Mark*

H.G. Bishop Mattaos
bishop and abbot of the Syrian monastery

Forward by his holiness
Father Mattaos
the bishop and abbot of the Syrian monastery

The first arabic edition of this book was in 1983, and it was soon sold out because of the important topic the book talks about, which is the miracle of moving the Mokattam Mountain and the great spiritual persons spoken of in it; such as the great Pope Abram Ibn Zaraa and Saint Samaan the Tanner.

And now the church of Saint Samaan the Shoemaker in Mokattam is so kind as to publish a second augmented and revised edition. To this edition a chapter was added dealing with the discovery of the remains of Samaan the Shoemaker.

The book has been made complete by the laborious efforts of the reverend priest fathers of the Saint Samaan church in Mokattam Mountain and the efforts of the fellow-ministers in the church.

To all these we acknowledge our debt and render our thanks, hoping that this book will be a cause of blessing and steadfastness in the orthodox, wonder-working faith for all those who read it.

May our holy Mother Saint Mary grant us her intercession, and may our Father Saint Abram Ibn Zaraa and the great Saint of faith and the performer of the miracle Samaan the Shoemaker grant us their prayers, together with our Honored Father H. H. Pope Shenouda III.

May the blessing of the Lord include us all. Amen.

__Bishop Mattaos__
__The Bishop and Abbot of__
__the Syrian monastery.__

The Coptic Orthodox church has immortalized the memory of the miracle of moving the Mokattam mountain, which was performed by Saint Samaan the Tanner, by observing the three day fast which the church kept at the time of the miracle. The church has appended these days to one of the holiest fasts of our church- the fast of the holy Christmas. The duration of the Christmas fast was forty days, but after the three day fast of this miracle was added to it, the sum total of the Christmas fast became 43 days, starting from November 25. and ending on January 6. of every year.

Nevertheless, no one has ever taken the pains to immortalize the memory of that great Saint, through whom the Lord performed this supernatural miracle. Many churches have been built for the memory of other Saints, such as Saint Girgis, Saint Mina, Saint Antonios, and many others. As for Saint Samaan the Tanner, no church was built in his name throughout the previous thousand years, until Providence chose to bring to memory the name of this Saint, which was carried out by building the first church in his name on the Mokattam Mountain itself in 1974 under H. H. Pope Shenouda III may God grant him long life.

Isn't it worthy that the whole world, and the Copts of Egypt in particular, should know the biography of this great Saint?

Here we present this stirring biography, and the account of the supernatural miracle of moving the Mokattam Mountain, together with the miracle of building the Church of Saint Samaan the Tanner in the Mokattam mountain.

May the blessing of the prayers of this great Saint, Samaan the Tanner, the prayers of all the Saints, and the prayers of our blessed father Pope Shenouda III be with us all. Amen.

The Church
January 15 .1994 AD
Saturday, Hatur 17.1710 AM
On the feast of Samaan the Tanner.

CHAPTER 1

THE TIME OF SAINT SAMAAN

1) The destroying famine.
2) The construction of Cairo.
3) Chaos in Tanis.
4) The settlement of peace.
5) Religious freedom.
6) The state of the church.

Saint Samaan the Tanner lived towards the end of the tenth century AD. He was a contemporary of the Saint Bishop Abram Ibn Zaraa the Syrian, who occupied the seat of St. Mark in 975 AD and rested in peace in 979 AD.

It is, therefore, preferable to take a passing look at the time during which the Saint lived, since the time and the place where we now live will, whether we like it or not, affect the way we see things, for the bible says: 'Do not be misled: **"Bad company corrupts good character."** (1 Co. 15:33). For the house in which a child grows up is like the soil that provides not only for his physical needs, but for his spiritual and psychological ones, as well. I wonder if every father and mother of us realizes the responsibility towards their children that is laid on their shoulders ? Or is it true that concern for the things of this present world; such as food, clothes, and earthly position has become our sole pre- occupation.

Yet, the wisest of men throughout the ages has announced, "Yet when I surveyed all that my hands had done and I had toiled to achieve, everything was meaningless, a chasing after the wind; nothing was gained under the sun." (Ecc. 2:11).

My Lord, Jesus Christ,
I ask You for help for the
responsibility and the trust
You have entrusted me
with.
Let me and my children
and all my household be
yours. Let our motto be
"But as for me and my
household we will serve
the Lord." (Jos. 24:15).
Lord, answer my
prayer and make my
reading of this moving
biography a blessing, a
cause of change in my
life, as I take it as my
example.. Amen.

1) THE DESTROYING FAMINE

A severe and overwhelming famine came upon all of Egypt under the reign of the Ikhshidid Empire, namely between AD 934 to AD 968, shortly before the Fatimid Empire was established, under which the miracle of moving the mountain took place. The miracle took place circa AD 979, so Saint Samaan must have lived through this famine, which sent more than half a million people to their early graves. (1)

Among the causes of this famine was a shortage in the annual inundation of the Nile for three consequent years. Consequently, epidemics spread and this large number of people died. Whole towns vanished, and dioceses just faded out of existence. (2)

These events must have left an impression on the Saint's soul and made him renounce pleasure in worldly things- as we shall see.

This was -and is- God's way of dealing with man...

My beloved brother, has God allowed some painful experiences to happen to you? Has life all around you closed up on you, while you are passing through its barren wilderness? Have you been unable to bear the heaviness and heat of the day for your human frailty ? Has resentment become your way of life, and have the words of your mouth become murmuring and complaining of the circumstances? Or do you see God in the scene and receive from Him all the circumstances, knowing that " all things work together for the good of those who love God " (Ro. 8:28)?

My friend, people are divided as their reactions to hard circumstances into three categories: the first murmurs against and resents the circumstances, and maybe God himself, while the second receives them in silence, and the third gives thanks even in the heated furnace, knowing that God will bring "out of the eater, something to eat; out of the strong, something sweet" (Jdg. 14:14). This third kind of person learns the lessons, and, therefore, comes out from the fire brighter than before; as Job the prophet of patience said, "When he has tested me, I shall come forth as gold." (Job 23:10) Of which category are you, and what is your reaction to the circumstances?

My loving God, I thank You with all my heart for all tribulation and all pain at all times. Grant me to adopt thanksgiving, for all circumstances and under all circumstances, as a

way of life, trusting that
You are able to use all
them to form my life as it
pleases You. Give me
patience during tribulation
and long-suffering at
times of trial. Amen.

2) THE CONSTRUCTION OF CAIRO

Cairo had been constructed only a short while before the miracle of moving the mountain took place. As a matter of fact, the present Cairo (3) is made up of several small, old towns that were built in different ages. One of these towns received the name **"Cairo"**.

These old towns are:

(A) **Babylon, or the Palace of Wax.** (It is now old Cairo. Was established by the Byzantines.)

(B) **Um Danin.** Is now in the center of Cairo, where the main train station is.

(C) **Al-Fustat**. Near Ain Al-Sira. Was established by Amru Ibn Al-As.

(D) **Al-Askar**. Between Al-Fustat and the Mokattam mountain.

(E) **Al-Qata`i.** In the vicinity of Al-Askar by Ibn Tulun's mosque. Was established by Ahmad Ibn Tulun.

(F) **Cairo.** Is the area where Al-Azhar mosque is. Was established by the Fatimids under Al-Mu'iz Li-Din Illah in AD 969. It was under this same monarch that the miracle of moving the Mokattam mountain occurred, which happened exactly ten years after Cairo was con- structed. As we shall see, there a connection between the city of Cairo and the miracle of moving the mountain.

3) CHAOS IN TANIS

Tanis is the present town of San in the Sharqia Governorate. The chaos that happened in it at the beginning Fatimid reign plucked the feeling of security from the hearts of the Copts and made them take refuge with God as their only protection in such events. Some extremists had risen against the government and against the Copts, and announced their independence, while some of them plundered the homes of the Christians and took their women and daughters as booty. Chaos reigned in that city until some Copts, the children of Qashlan by name, were able to contact the government and stop these insurrections. (4).

No doubt that these incidents had a great effect on the souls of the believers, for in calamities hearts are turned towards God and the people's commitment to the church increases.

4) THE SETTLEMENT OF PEACE

After these incidents, and thanks to the wisdom of Al-Mu'iz Li Din Illah the Fatimid, security was realized in the country, and peace prevailed throughout Egypt.

This was reflected on the souls of the citizens, and the voices of the believers were raised in thanksgiving to God the Prince of peace for the peace he bestowed on them.

5) RELIGIOUS FREEDOM

Al-Mu'iz Li Din Illah the Fatimid, who reigned from AD 969 till the end of AD 979, was a polished politician, besides being a letterman and a lover of the gatherings in which poetry was recited. He was, as well, fond of religious sciences, which made him invite the Muslim, the Christian, and the Jewish religious leaders in order to debate before him with all frankness and freedom, and without any anger or contention.

This matter has a direct relationship with the miracle of moving the Mokattam mountain, as we shall see later on.

6) Handicrafts

The Copts worked in all kinds of crafts and professions; such as carpentry, construction of furniture, smithery and ship making. They even celebrated Mass on the decks of their boats at the ports officially (5), because all the workers, craftsmen, and even the sailors were Copts.

We shall see, therefore, that Saint Samaan the Tanner worked in one of these handicrafts, which was tanning the hides of animals.

7) THE STATE OF THE CHURCH

Due to the peace that reigned over the country under the Fatimid empire, the Copts neglected the election of a new Patriarch for the church for two years, from the death of Pope Mina II in AD 973 till AD 975.

The bishops and the archdeacons later gathered in the church of Abu Sirga in Old Cairo in order to discuss who was fitting for the patriarchy. Thereupon, a righteous, respected, and pious old man came in, who was known to all of them named Abram Ibn Zaraa the Syrian. Now this man was also a friend of the Fatimid caliph Al-Mu'iz Li Din Illah. The multitudes, therefore, elected him unanimously as patriarch in the month of Tuba 687AM, January AD.

After his ordination as patriarch, he distributed all his possessions to the poor and the needy, and to the churches and the monasteries. He also forbade simony and opposed an evil habit that prevailed amongst the Christians, namely the possession of concubines.

In   general, the church at his time was in a blessed age of spiritual revival.

Lord, I thank You for my beloved Mother the Church, in which You planted me, so that I might be nourished by Your holy word, and grow steadfast in this vineyard which Your right arm has planted. I thank You because You hasten Your word to perform it. I thank You because You established Your church on the rock and the gates of Hell shall not prevail against it. I thank You for my fathers the Saints, the pillars of the church. Teach me to consider the end of their lives and emulate their faith.

CHAPTER 2

GLIMPSES INTO THE LIFE OF SAINT SAMAAN THE TANNER

1) His upbringing
2) His profession.
3) His purity.
4) His abstinence and asceticism.
5) the depth of his devotion (A man of prayer).
6) His practical service.
7) His amazing humility.
8) His strong faith.
9) His end.

1) HIS UPBRINGING

This Saint appeared suddenly on the scene of historical events as a shining star, and disappeared just the same way. History does not mention anything about his early upbringing at all, so we do not know where he was born, or where he was reared up, or who was his father.

Butfor the will of the Lord that made him appear for the performing of this miracle and the delivering of this message, we would not have heard about him at all! This proves that there are many Saints of the Lord whom the world does not know. They are hidden from sight. Wasn't this been the case at the time of Elijah the prophet?! Didn't this same prophet say to the Lord, "I am the only one left." (1 ki 19:10)?! What did the Lord answer him? Did not He say, "Yet I reserve seven thousand in Israel- all whose knees have not bowed down to Baal and all whose mouths have not kissed him." (1 Ki 19:18)?!

How amazing! Seven thousand persons for the Lord, and Elijah himself did not know about them!

The people are not all bad, my beloved brother. Look around you; maybe the Lord will reveal to you many Saints, whom you cannot otherwise see.

Saint Samaan the Tanner was one of the obscure Saints- hidden away from sight. And even though we know nothing of his birth, yet history asserts he was in Babylon (Old Cairo) during the time of Pope Abram the Syrian (AD 975-979), which was under Al-Mu'iz Li Din Illah, the first ruler in the Fatimid dynasty in Egypt.

My dear God, I thank You for the cloud of Saints which fills Your beloved Church. I thank You because You do not leave yourself without a witness; but rather have children and holy men in every generation. Protect me from the spirit of despair which fought the courageous prophet Elijah in old times to the point that he sought death for his soul. Lord, make me steadfast in hope because You have not given us the spirit of fear, but the spirit of love, help, and self-control. Amen.

2) HIS PROFESSION

At that time the Copts were engaged in handicrafts, as we have mentioned above. Saint Samaan, therefore, worked also in one of the crafts that were widespread in Babylon (Old Cairo), which was tanning. (Old Cairo is still known for this craft today.)

Most probably, this profession was not confined in the past to tanning animal skins, but included also the crafts that depend on this process, such as shoemaking and the like.

Our Saint carried several titles related to skins, of which we list the following:

Samaan the Tanner. (6)
Samaan the Cobbler. (7)
Samaan the shoemaker. (8)

This was also the profession of Saint Ananaias the first patriarch of the Coptic church after St. Mark. The latter, after having traveled about in Alexandria, went to this cobbler to mend his torn shoes. And when the awl pierced through the hand of the cobbler, he cried out, "Ious theos," which means "O the One God."

St. Mark used this exclamation to evangelize the cobbler, who believed on the Lord Jesus Christ, and was later ordained a patriarch to lead the church after St. Mark.

My Lord Jesus Christ, I thank You for the profession that you gave me. Thanks for the mind that you created in me to learn this profession. Lord, allow me to use it for your glory, so that Your great name might be exalted by it, as it is exalted in everything You created. Grant me true Christian honesty in practicing this profession, so that people may see my good works and glorify our father who is in heaven. Amen.

3) HIS PURITY

When the Saint was practicing his work as a shoemaker, a woman came to him to mend her shoes, and this woman was beautiful. It so happened that when she was taking off her shoes, her legs showed and he looked lustfully at her. But at once he drove the awl into one of his eyes, thus plucking it out (9) in keeping with the commandment of the Lord "But I tell you that anyone who looks at a woman lustfully has committed adultery with her i his heart. If your right eye causes you to sin, gouge it and throw it away. It is better for you to lose one part of your body than for your whole body to be thrown into hell." (Mt. 5:28,29).

Yes, how beautiful the history of the church is, with all its narratives about the Saintly fathers. It follows the same pattern which the Bible adopted in narrating the lives of its Saints. Before mentioning their strength, it mentions their human weakness, to which the power of Christ comes and changes it into strength, and thus life is brought forth from death, and satisfying honey from the dead lion.

Hasn't the Bible mentioned the sin of lying in the life of Abraham the father of faith (Gen 12:13), and the sin of adultery in the life of David (2 Sa 11)? Even the apostle Paul himself, being our teacher, has declared this very clearly when he said, "Even though I was once a blasphemer and a persecutor and a violent man, I was shown mercy because I acted in ignorance and unbelief." (1 Ti 1:13). Yes, my dear brother, how wonderful the grace of Christ is, which lifts up from weakness and empowers with strength; and it even draws people out of the dunghill and seats them on thrones.

St. Samaan simply carried out the commandment literally. the great scholar Oregon had done a similar thing before him when he castrated himself in fulfillment of the verse that says: "Others have renounced marriage (or castrated themselves) because of the kingdom of heaven." (Mt 19:12). Each one of them has so acted in total sincerity to carry out the commandment literally, even though the church does not allow this, not to mention teach it. It was nothing but a literal and simple act which the church tolerated. But when Oregon castrated himself, the church excommunicated him, in spite of his status as great scholar, for the Lord did not mean it to be taken literally, but He was rather pointing to the mortification of the flesh; as the church teaches us to pray, saying, "Mortify our physical senses, O Christ our God." This is the same thing that the apostle Paul meant when he said, "Count yourselves dead to sin." (Ro 6:11).

My Lord Jesus Christ, I thank You for these bright, holy, pure models that hate evil. Yes, it was You who made them hate evil ... Give me belief in Your existence in my heart, which is able to transform the corruption of my life into a life of purity. You can replace what the locusts of uncleanness have eaten with a life of holiness. Lord, grant me to submit to the Spirit of holiness, so that he might work in me His holy works, and break off all the bonds of my sins through the intercession of Saint Samaan the Tanner, the example of the life of holiness.. Amen.

4) His abstinence and asceticism

Saint Samaan the Tanner was an ascetic person, which fact was made known from the conversation he had with the patriarch Abram, when the latter asked him about his life when The Virgin Mary led him to meet him. He said about himself,

"I eat a little just to keep myself alive." (10)

Thus we can see how this Saint renounced the pleasures of this life, contenting himself with the least, so as to keep himself alive!

Having control over the lust of the stomach by abstaining from food is one of the characteristics of asceticism, and also a sign of practical holiness. Therefore we hear of the Saint Anba Bola the Anchorite that his food consisted of half a loaf of bread which a crow carried him. Saint Sara says, **"A mouth that You keep from water does not ask for wine, and a stomach that You keep from bread does not ask for meat."**

One further sign of his asceticism was the way he dressed. For on the day of the miracle, he went to the mountain together with the Patriarch, the bishops, the priests, the multitudes of the people, and the secular celebrities in his shabby clothes (11) [which were his usual clothes that he wore when he went to the tannery].

We do not want to say that uncleanness is a sign of holiness, as Pope wears very expensive clothes, especially during Feasts! but we say that not adorning oneself and not wearing expensive clothes (1 Ti 2:9) is a sign of the children of God.

So then, Saint Samaan the Tanner, as far as pious life is concerned, was ascetic in his clothes and food as were many of our father Saints; such as Saint Bola, Saint Ruweis, Saint Barsum the naked, and others.

Does not this show us another aspect of power, which is the power of the Holy Spirit of God which is different from the power of the flesh and the appearance? Doesn't this remind us of Saint John the Baptist who used to wear camel's hair and eat honey and wild locusts? In spite of this, the Bible says, "Because Herod feared John and protected him, knowing him to be a righteous and holy man. When Herod heard John, he was greatly puzzled; yet he liked to listen to him." (Mk 6:20). And likewise Saint Samaan the Tanner did not fix his eyes on what is seen, but on what is unseen. For what is seen is temporary, but what is unseen is eternal. (2 Co 4:18).

5) THE DEPTH OF HIS DEVOTION (A MAN OF PRAYER)

The secret of the blessing in the life of Saint Sámaan the Tanner lay in the fact that he was a wonderful man of prayer. For he showed in his secret conversation with the Pope that he spent long hours in prayer. He said, **"And at sunset I go out with the rest of the wage workers and eat just a little, so as to keep myself barely alive. Then I turn to prayer, and stand the whole night praying."** (13)

Prayer is the secret of blessing in the life of the Saints, for it brings loving fellowship between the believer and his God. Therefore, the good pleasure of the believer is to spend his time in the presence of God. It was the lifestyle of the Lord Jesus in his humanity on earth, for the Scripture says: "Very early in the morning, while it was still dark, Jesus got up, left the house and went off to a solitary place, where he prayed." (Mk 1:35) It says also: "One of these days Jesus went out to a mountain to pray, and spent the night praying to God." (Lk 6:12) David also teaches us, saying, "But I am a man of prayer." (Ps 109:4) Likewise, Mary enjoyed sitting at Jesus' feet, **"choosing what is better, which will not be taken away from her."** (Lk 10:42).

In fact, when the beauty of the Lord is revealed to the believer, he cannot bear to live without fixing his gaze upon that beauty, therefore David says, "One thing I ask of the Lord, this is what I seek: that I may dwell in the house of the Lord all the days of my life to gaze upon the beauty of the Lord and to seek him in his temple." (Ps 27:4)

In these terms, Saint Arsenius used to spend the whole night in prayer, just as Saint Samaan the Tanner was a man of prayer, for he enjoyed the depth of the fellowship with God.

My Lord Jesus, how I do need to start this blessed communion with You in the life of prayer, as my father Saints have live it ! Please, my beloved Lord, make me love to sit with You and open my eyes to the wonder of the true communion and the transcendence of the spiritual blessings which I

will enjoy in Your presence.
Raise my soul up from its
laziness, and revive it from
its sleep of weakness to the
blessed struggle of prayer.
Amen.

6) HIS PRACTICAL SERVICES

One of the secrets that Saint Samaan the Tanner revealed during his conversation with Anba Abram was the fact that he ministered to the older people and the sick, bringing them water every day. He said, **"I wake up as early as this hour in the morning every day to fill my jar with water and distribute it to the elderly and the sick, who have been hampered from bringing water for themselves by old age or sickness. When I am finished with this service of mine, I return my water skin to the house and go to my work..."** (14)

This ministry which Saint Samaan the Tanner used to do was one of the ministries that people would tend to depreciate and despise. While in fact it was such a great service of which the Lord said, "And if anyone gives even a cup of cold water to one of these little ones because he is my disciple, I tell the truth, he will not lose his reward." (Mt 10:42)

Many people concern themselves with the big, manifest ministries, but the humble choose the little despicable ones, and do them for the Lord.

Besides distributing water to those people, Saint Samaan also used to **"distribute everyday bread and food to the cloistered hermits, whether of men or women." (15)**

So Samaan the Tanner was a full-fledged Saint!

7) HIS AMAZING HUMILITY

Saint Samaan was so humble, and we can see the marks of his humility in the following occurrences:

(A) When the Virgin Mary revealed his holiness to the Pope, and he went out to get him in order to perform the miracle, Samaan the tanner said to him, **"Forgive me, father; I am but a sinful man." (16)**

37

What a profound statement that denotes the depth of his humility. It is the language of the Saints: "Forgive me", "I am a sinful man." Doesn't this remind us of what our teacher Peter said to the Lord Jesus: **"Go away from me, Lord; for I am a sinful man."** (Lk 5:8) and of what our teacher Paul said: **"Christ Jesus came to this world to save sinners-of whom I am the worst."** (1 Ti 1:15)?

(B) When the Pope asked him to tell him a little about his life, he was obliged to tell him his story, but at the conclusion he "besought him to keep it secret as long as he lived on this earth." (17) He also said to him, "I beg you my father not to expose me to anyone, for I have no power to bear the glory of men." (18)

This Saint had learnt humility from the gentle and humble Master who said to his disciples, "I do not accept praise from men." (John 5:41) he, therefore, said His disciples, "Do not tell anyone what you have seen, until the Son of Man has been raised from the dead." (Mt17:9)

(C) The humility of Saint Samaan the Tanner appears also, when the Pope asked him to perform the miracle, while Saint Samaan stood among the people behind him, and he said to him, **"So that no one would recognize me."** (19)

Thus, Saint Samaan stood among the common people while the miracle was being performed and uttered not a word or showed any sign or movement indicating that it was he who performed the miracle, so as not to draw attention to himself!!

What an amazing humility!!

(D) Another sign of his humility was that, after the miracle had been performed ,**"the Pope turned left and right looking for Samaan the Tanner, but he was nowhere to be found, and none has ever found him after that."** (20)

Where had he gone?! Had he disappeared willingly, so that he might let no man have any hope in his appearance anymore and thus be exposed to receive vain praise from people?

It is the life of amazing humility that seeks the glory of Christ, and not its own; the life that has adopted the motto: "He must become greater; I must become less." (John 3:30)

O how do I need, my great Lord, to live the life of humility, learning from You,

my Lord, for You are gentle
and humble in heart, so that
I may find rest for my soul!
O Lord, how often I sought
my own glory! But let me de-
crease so that You may
increase and be lifted up and
exalted. O my Lord, keep me
from the arrows of vainglory,
for I am the unworthy
servant. Help me to start
from now.. Amen.

8) HIS STRONG FAITH

The time when sadness was sweeping over the church, and perplexity filled the heart of Pope Abram (21), Saint Samaan was steadfast and assured of the Lord's powers and the might of His strength. For he said to the Pope, **" My honorable father, go up the mountain that the caliph tells you, and you shall see the glory of God."** (22)

It was all according to his faith. The miracle was achieved and the mountain was moved from its place, because he trusted in the promise of the Lord that says,

"If you have faith as small as a mustard seed, you can say to this mountain, `Move from here to there,' and it will move. Nothing will be impossible for you." (Mt 17:20)

This is an example of the lives of our Saint fathers "who through faith conquered kingdoms, administered justice, and gained what was promised; who shut the mouths of lions, quenched the fury of the flames, and escaped the edge of the sword; whose weakness was turned to strength; and who became powerful in battle and routed foreign armies... the world was not worthy of them." (Heb 11:33,34,38)

9) HIS END

This Saint, as we have said earlier, was like a bright star that glimmered all of a sudden, and disappeared just the same way. History recorded his end after this fashion:

It was natural that this miracle would cause quite a commotion in the ranks of all those who witnessed it.

When they calmed down, and gained their composure back, they began to go down the mountain, going back to their homes. His felicity the Patriarch looked right and left searching for Samaan the Tanner, but he was nowhere to be found, and none has found him ever after. (23)

Yet, the Lord, in His great love, has revealed the body of this great Saint, as we shall see later on.

Lord, I thank You for this shining life of which I have just read. I pray You, my God, to turn these words which I have read into life for me to live, and place inside me holy longings to live these blessed qualities which You have given that great man of faith, Saint Samaan the Tanner.. in his intercession I pray. Amen.

CHAPTER 3

THE MIRACLE OF THE MOVING OF THE MOKATTAM MOUNTAIN

1) The incidents that pave the way for the miracle.
2) The distress is dispersed.
3) The supernatural miracle.
4) The results of the miracle.
5) Recording the miracle.
6) A research on the determination of the date of the miracle.

1) THE INCIDENTS THAT PAVE THE WAY FOR THE MIRACLE

1) Heated religious discussion:

As we said earlier, Al-Mu'iz Li Din-Illah the Fatimid was fond of literary gatherings and much interested in religious controversies. He used to rally the religious leaders of the Muslims, the Christians and the Jews and let them debate in his presence, and stipulated that this should be carried out with neither anger nor contention.

There was a Jew in the retinue of Al-Mu'iz who espoused Islam in order to be assigned a minister. This man's name was Jacob Ibn Killis.

In spite of the fact that he espoused Islam, he still sided with Judaism, because he did not adopt Islam out of belief in it, but for the sake of the governmental office. Now this Jew hated Christians very much, especially because he had a Christian rival who was dear to the caliph. This Jew feared that the caliph would appoint the christian as minister instead of him. This man's name was Quzman Ibn Mina, and had the title "Abul Yumn" (The fortunate one).

So, Jacob Ibn Killis the Jew called to him another Jew named Moses and wanted him to debate with the Patriarch Abram in the court of the caliph Al-Mu'iz.

The caliph sent a message to the Patriarch, saying, "If you want to debate the Jews someday, whether yourself or through one of the bishops you choose, come to my house and join issue with them in my presence."

So Pope Abram set a date for the debate, and took along with him Anba Sawirus Ibn Al-Muqaffaa the bishop of Ashmunin (in Upper Egypt), who was one of the church scholars in his generation. It was he who wrote **"THE BIOGRAPHY OF THE PATRIARCHS,"** and besides this he was well versed in theology, especially in comparative religion, and authored numerous volumes in this field. Of these books are: **A BOOK ON MONOTHEISM, and THE BOOK OF THE WONDROUS PRESENTATION IN ANSWER TO THE JEWS,** among other books.

When the caliph was seated, together with the Jewish minister Ibn Killis and his friend Moses, he said to the Pope,

"Speak my reverent Pope, or otherwise grant your companions the permission to talk."

So the Pope said to Sawirus the bishop of Ashmunin,

"Speak my son, and the divine wisdom grant you wisdom."

Anba Sawirus said in spiritual prudence,

"It is not proper to address a Jew in the presence of the caliph."

Moses, the minister's companion, was enraged and said,

"You are insulting me in the hearing of the prince of the believers [the title of the caliph among Muslims], since you describe me as ignorant."

Anba Sawirus asked him calmly,

"What if I furnish the proof for your ignorance, will you not be angry?"

The caliph interfered out of tolerance, and eloquently,

"There is no need to be angry in the discussion; freedom is vouchsafed for each of you so that you may express each his own opinion frankly and without embarrassment."

Anba Sawirus said confidently,

"Well, it is not I that call you ignorant; it is rather a great prophet of yours, who had a special favor from God, who witnesses against you."

Moses the Jew asked him,

"And who can this prophet be?"

Anba Sawirus answered immediately,

"It is Isaiah the prophet, who said about you, `The ox knows his master, the donkey, his owner's manger, but Israel does not know, my people do not understand.'" (Is 1:3)

The caliph burst out laughing , for he was impressed by Anba Sawirus' prudence and skill of speech. Then the caliph asked Moses the Jew,

"Are these really the words of Isaiah?"

Moses said, with pent-up anger,

"Yes, sire."

And Anba Sawirus continued talking,

"Behold a great prophet of yours has announced that the animals have more understanding that you do."

The caliph was still under the intoxicating effect of the brilliance of this joke, and decided to end the session, having heard enough for the day.

2) The malicious plot :

This sharp debate upset the minister Ibn Killis and his other Jewish companion Moses so much that they decided to take revenge on Anba Abram and Anba Sawirus by devising a plot that would destroy the Copts altogether. For this reason, the Jew started to search the New Testament looking for something to help him in his malicious purpose. He chanced upon the verse that the Lord Jesus has said in Mt 17:20, which says: **"If you** have faith as small as a mustard seed, you can say to this mountain, `Move from here to there,' and it will move. Nothing will be impossible for you."

Moses the Jew and the minister Ibn Killis hastened to the caliph Al-Mu'iz and said to him,

"We have found it written in the book of the Christians that whosoever has faith as small as a mustard seed can move a mountain. So it is our right to demand them to prove that their religion is right by means of this. If they cannot, they should be punished for the invalidity of their religion."

The caliph kept silent and was mulling over this verse, thinking to himself that if the words of the New Testament were true, then this would be a golden opportunity to remove the mountain that was perched to the east of the new city (Cairo) so that it could stretch further east and would enjoy a terrific site, since the mountain was bordering Birket Elphil before it got removed. (24) But if they proved unable to carry this out, this would be a cogent proof that the religion of the Christians was wrong, so should be done away with completely.

The caliph Al-Mu'iz sent for Anba Abram the Syrian, who came to him and talked with him concerning this verse. He told him that he had to choose between these four alternatives: (25)

1) **To fulfill this commandment and move the eastern part of the Mokattam.**

2) **To espouse Islam and abandon Christianity on the account that it is invalid.**

3) **To leave Egypt and immigrate to another country.**

4) **To be smitten by the sword altogether.** (26)

The Patriarch kept silent, and was praying in his heart for the Lord to guide him in this ordeal.. Then he asked the caliph to give a three day respite, after which he would give him an answer.

3) Calling for a fast:

The Pope was very unhappy when he returned to his seat, and issued a public statement ordering all the Christians in Egypt to fast for three days from down, till sunset, and to lift up fervent prayers for the safety of the church, that God might deliver it from the impending ordeal. What a spiritual insight and heavenly wisdom is that which turns to God in such hard circumstances and distresses! How wonderful is the prayer of the church which it lifts up during the Mass, saying, **"For we do not know another but You...Your holy name is the name** we utter and our souls are revived by Your Holy Spirit."

Thereafter, the Pope went to the famous church of Saint Mary, which is know as "The Suspended Church," and called for the bishops who were present in Old Cairo, together with the archdeacons and the monks to tell them what had happened between the caliph and himself. He said to them,

"We are to fast and pray these three days which I have asked of the caliph as respite, so that the Lord may show mercy upon us in His grace, and provide us a way of deliverance."

All the people responded to the calling of the Pope, and the Coptic people fasted throughout the land of Egypt. Masses were held and prayers and supplications for this ordeal through which the church was going.

Pope Anba Abram, together with some bishops, priests, monks and archdeacons confined themselves to the Suspended Church of Saint Mary during those three days.

2) THE DISTRESS IS DISPERSED

1) The Virgin Mary appears to the Pope:

The third day at dawn, the Pope dozes off for a short while, saw the Virgin Mary, and heard her say to him,

"What is the matter with you?"

The Pope answered,

"You know, lady of the heavenly and earthly beings."

She said to him,

"Fear not, faithful shepherd, ... for your tears which you have shed in this church, and the fasts and the prayers which you and your people have offered up shall not be forgotten. Now, get out through the iron gate that leads to the market-place and, when you are on your way out, you will find a one-eyed man in front of you carrying a jar of water. Take hold of him; for he is the man by whom the miracle will take place."

As soon as the Virgin Mary said this, she was hidden from the sight of the Pope, who woke up from his sleep wondering.

2) Saint Samaan, the messenger of heaven:

When the Pope went out to the iron gate that leads to the market-place, and saw outside it the man whom the Virgin Mary had spoken, he took hold of him... brought him inside the iron gate, and closed it... The Pope told him what had happened between the caliph and himself, and what the Virgin Mary had ordered him to do, mentioning that it was he by whom the miracle would take place.

Saint Samaan said to him,

"Forgive me, my father, for I am but a sinful man."

The Pope said to him in persistence,

"It is the command of the mother of Light."

Saint Samaan answered in humility and submission,

"As long as it is the Mother of Light who decided that I should be entrusted with this great task, I, then, place myself at the you service, sir."

The Pope asked him about his name, and why he was there in the market-place at such an early hour in the morning while people are asleep.

Saint Samaan answered, **"My name is Samaan the Tanner. I work in tanning animal skins. But I wake up as early as this hour in the morning every** day to fill my jar with water and distribute it to the elderly and the sick, who have been hampered from bringing water for themselves by old age or sickness.

When I am finished with this service of mine, I return my water skin to the house and go to my work at the tannery where I work till evening. And at sunset I go out with the rest of the wage workers and eat just a little, so as to keep myself barely alive. Then I turn to prayer..."

Saint Samaan urged the Pope to keep the true state of his affairs hidden as long as he lived on this earth.

3) The preparations for the miracle :

After Saint Samaan had finished this, he said to the Patriarch,

"My honorable father, go up the mountain and take along with you the religious leaders, the deacons, and the archdeacons, and make them carry on high the Bibles, the crosses, and the long candles, these being lit, and the censers full of incense."

"And ask the king and his retinue to go up with you... So you shall stand on one side of the mountain, while they stand on the side opposite you. As for me, I will stand among the people behind your felicity, so that no one would recognize me.

"Then after administering the holy sacraments, you raise up your voice with all of the people, repeating, **"Kyrie Eleison" (have mercy, Lord)** four hundred times.

"Then after that keep silent for some moments, and worship, you and the priests, before the Most High. Repeat this three times, and every time you stand up after worshipping, draw the sign of the cross over the mountain, and you shall see the glory of God."

The Patriarch lifted up a prayer of thanksgiving to God, who allowed the trial to come, but provided a way out . (1 Co 10:13)

3) THE SUPERNATURAL MIRACLE

1) A great crowd of people:

The Patriarch told the caliph Al-Mu'iz Li Din Illah that he was ready to carry out his request by the grace of God... the caliph went out on the back of his steed, having with him several men of his retinue, his great men of honor, and his soldiers. He met the Patriarch and a great number of bishops, priests, deacons, archdeacons, the common people, and among these was Saint Samaan

the Tanner... The two parties stood opposite one another
on the mountain as Saint Samaan told them.

2) A great quake and the moving of the mountain:

After administering the holy sacraments which the
Pope and the bishops lifted up, the people repeated with
a broken spirit and a crushed heart the **"Kyrie Eleison"**
(heve mercy, Lord) prayer, four hundred times; 100 to
the east, another to the west, another to the north, and
another to the south.

Then they kept silent for a moment between the
hands of the Most High... And they started to worship
and stand up three times, while the Patriarch drew the
sign of the cross. And behold a great earthquake swept
over the mountain, and at each worship the mountain
was thrust down, and every time they stood up the
mountain would rise up and the sun would be seen from
under it. And every time it would go back to its
place.(27)

This was the power of faith which our teacher Paul
declared when he said, "I can do everything through him
who gives me strength." (Phil 4:13)

3) The caliph and the crowds become frightened:

When the miracle took place, the caliph Al-Mu'iz panicked and feared, together with all the multitudes that gathered with him; he cried out at the top of his voice,

"God is great; may His name be blessed."

And he entreated the Pope to stop what he was doing, otherwise the city would be overthrown.

When the things calmed down once more, he said to the Pope,

"You have proven that your faith is a true one. "

4) The disappearance of Saint Samaan:

After the souls of the gathered crowd calmed down, they began to come down the mountain and go back to their homes.

As for the Patriarch, he looked round about him searching for Saint Samaan the Tanner, who had been standing behind him, but he was nowhere to be found, and noone has found him ever again .. until the grace of God revealed him afterward, as we shall see.

5) calling the mountain Al-Mokattam:

A manuscript in the monastery of Anba Antonios relates that the Mokattam mountain was thus called because its surface was level and connected, but it became divided into three parts; one after the other, having a space in between. (28)

The Arabic dictionaries say that the word **"Mokattam"** means **"cut up."** (29)

4) THE RESULTS OF THE MIRACLE

This mighty miracle had many important results, of which we list the following:

1) Renewing and restoring the churches:

After the miracle had been performed, the caliph Al-Mu'iz Li Din Illah took the Pope aside and spoke to him privately, saying,

"Now, ask whatever you want and we will do it for you."

The Pope answered wisely,

"The only thing I ask is that the Lord may lengthen your span of life, and give you victory over your enemies."

The caliph, however, insisted that the pope should ask something, so the Patriarch said,

"Since you press me to reveal my desire to you, allow me to say that I desire that the church of Saint Markorios Abu Sifein (Babylon, Old Cairo) be rebuilt;

for some mob and riffraff had it torn down, and used what was left of it as a storehouse for sugar-cane. Also I would like the walls of the Suspended Church to be restored, for they are now cracked."

As soon as the caliph heard these requests, he ordered a clerk in his office to draw up a decree immediately that would grant the Patriarch the right to do whatever he asked of the caliph.

He commanded that all the expenses be provided for from the state treasury... The Pope took the decree that entitled him to build and restore the church, but apologized for not taking the money, and said to the caliph,

"The One for whom we are building the church is able to help us complete it; he is in no need of the money of the world."

The church was rebuilt.

It is an example of the life of contentedness and satisfaction with one's portion that Anba Abram did not ask the caliph for any personal need or possessions.

The renewal of the church of Markorios Abu Sifein was a herald of a new age of building and renewal. A great number of churches were restored, especially in Alexandria.

2) The peace of the Church:

The miracle of moving the Mokattam Mountain had a profound effect on all people, and the fear of the Lord fell upon all the people in the country, big and small, for history records this, saying:

> *Peace replaced upheaval and war. And Anba Abram's heart was full of assurance toward his faithful people.. (30)*

One of the reasons why peace prevailed in the church was due to what was said about the caliph himself... (31)

This reminds us of what happened with the Emperor of the Roman empire Constantine the Great, who, after seeing the sign of the cross in his sleep, and realizing victory in his battles, believed in Christ.

There is nothing too difficult for the Lord, for the grace of God can enter into the courts of kings and emperors; taking captivity captives and giving gift unto men. Our teacher the apostle Paul wrote, "All the Saints send you greetings, especially those who belong to Caesar's household." (Phil 4"22)

5) RECORDING THE MIRACLE

Providence willed it that this miracle should be eternalized down the ages and remain intact in the intellect of the people, untainted by the years and undiminished by the forgetfulness of man. It remains a witness to God's glory and surpassing power that can shake and move mountains. This miracle will tell every generation that the gates of hell shall not prevail against the church of God, and that every weapon that was formed against it shall not prosper...

H. H. Pope Shenouda III has reflected all these meanings in his poem "FOR THE CHURCH" of which we quote the following excerpt:

The gates of hell shall not prevail against you,
So rest assured and relax , for the One crucified is with you.
Ask about the time of Al-Mu'iz, for it knows it out of experience;
Ask it how by faith you moved the Mokattam,
A mountain that shook because of you, and you willed it,
You could break into pieces.

You who forget, understand the heart of history.

The means whereby this miracle was immortalized are:

1) The three day fast that precedes the Christmas fast:

The Pope Anba Abram the Syrian decided to make the three days which the church fasted on account of this miracle as a continuing ordinance in the church, which all the Copts should keep. After these three days were added to the Christmas fast, it became 43 days after it has once been 40 only. It begins on November 25. each year.

Here is what history has to say about it:

Anba Abram has appended three days to the Christmas fast, which used to be forty days; these three days being the days which the Christians fasted under that Patriarch to remove the impending flail from them which came about because of the wiles of the Jewish minister Jacob Ibn Killis. (23)

2) The icon of the two Saints, Anba Abram and Samaan the Tanner:

An icon adorns the northern wall in the yard of the church of The Virgin Mary, which is known as *"The Suspended Church"*, in Old Cairo that dates back to the fifteenth century AD (which is five centuries after the miracle, and it must have been drawn from another picture that we do not have at present). This icon represents Anba Abram and Saint Samaan the Tanner, and together with them the Virgin Mary appears in the picture. (33)

3) The building of a church in the name of Saint Samaan the Tanner in the Mokattam Mountain:

The will of God decreed that the first church would be built in the memory of this miracle after ten centuries of its occurrence. It was built on the Mokattam itself under H. H. Pope Shenouda III in 1974, as we shall see later on.

6) A RESEARCH ON THE DETERMINATION OF THE DATE OF THE MIRACLE

History has recorded the miracle of moving the Mokattam mountain showing that it took place under the caliph Al-Mu'iz Li Din Illah Al-Fatimi, which coincides with the time of Pope Abram the Syrian the 62nd. Patriarch, at the hands of Saint Samaan the Tanner.

But history does not record the day, the month, and the year in which the miracle was performed, which is a remarkable thing indeed!

Maybe the reason for this neglect is the fact that the miracle was such a supernatural occurrence to the historians of that era that they deemed it superfluous to back it up historically, for *on that day an unforgettable earthquake shook the earth,* and it was kept in people's minds by the power of its effect that shook the souls. So it was meant to remain intact in the minds, down the ages...

But forgetfulness is human, therefore history is found lacking in the determination of the date of the miracle.

In fact, it is not difficult to know the exact day, month, and year of the miracle, for we can get to know that by comparing the events that occurred at the time of the miracle. This we shall try to clarify in our research, by the grace of God and the wisdom of the Holy Spirit.

1) Determining the year of the miracle:

In order to be able to deduce the year in which the miracle took place, let us review the following:

(A) The miracle must have happened between the years 975 and 979 AD.

The miracle was performed under Pope Abram The Syrian who was ordained as patriarch in AD 975 and rested in peace in AD 979. So the miracle should be restricted to these two dates.

(B) The miracle must have happened in the same year of the renewal of the church of Abu Sifein:

The renewal of this church was one of the results of the miracle. When the caliph insisted the Pope should ask for him something which he (the caliph) promised to carry out, the Pope asked for a permission to renew the church of Markorios Abu Sifein in Old Cairo.

History says:

And he ordered, immediately, that a legal paper of entitlement should be written him... **(34)**

And it also says:

The caliph commanded that he should be given the church of Abu Sifein right away (35)

The word *"immediately"* and the word "right away" indicate that the permission to renew the church took place directly after the miracle, namely in the same year of the miracle.

It is well established from history that the renewal of the church had begun also at the time of the miracle, namely shortly after the permission was issued and the church was handed over. Our evidence of this is the historical record of the events that occurred at the beginning of the renewal of the church.

When the decree that Al-Mu'iz issued was read in front of the church of Abu Sifein, the mobs gathered in clamor and objection, declaring that they would not allow anyone to rebuild the church.

The caliph heard of what had happened,
and got furiously angry to the extent that he
rode his steed and headed his army to Babylon,
to the spot where Anba Abram wanted to work.

As soon as he arrived there, he ordered the
builders to work in his presence and under his
own supervision. When the mobs saw how firm
the caliph Al-Mu'iz was, they stood there in
silence and just looked at him as if stricken
with awe. (36)

These facts confirm that the building of the church
of Abu Sifein was started directly after the miracle, for
the caliph was still so impressed and enthusiastic that he
himself came in order to enable the pope to work on the
building.

It is a historical fact that the rebuilding of the
Markorios Abu Sifein church was in AD 979.(37)

(C) Then the year the miracle took
placemust have been AD 979:

This is because the year of the rebuilding of the
church of Markorios Abu Sifein is supposed to have
followed the miracle directly.

2) Determining the day of the miracle:

(A) It is an established historical fact that the Patriarch Anba Abram called for a three day fast for the miracle to happen, saying to the bishops, the priests and the people whom he gathered in the Suspended Church:

"We are to fast and pray these three days which I have asked of the caliph as respite, so that the Lord may show mercy upon us in His grace, and provide us a way of deliverance."
(38)

(B) It is also estabished historically that in the third day of the fast, the miracle happened ... for it is recorded that " *In the morning of the third day the Patriarch told the Caliph that he was going to move the Mountain .. "* (39)

(C) It is also known historically that these three days of fasting were added to the Christmas fast, for it is recorded that *"three days were appended to the Christmas fast, which used to be forty days only... These three days are the days which the Christians fasted under the Patriarch to remove the impending flail from them which came about because of the wiles of the Jewish minister."* (40)

68

(D) The question that concerns us here is why this three day fast of the miracle was added to the Christmas fast in particular?

Has this been done haphazardly, irrationally?

But how could we conceive it has been so done?

And could the church accept such an act?

Then, there must be a reason and a relationship between these three days and the Christmas fast.

(E) If it were up to the church to append these days to any other fast, it would have rather added it to the fast of Jonah or the fast of the Virgin; and this is for the following reasons:

1) The addition to the fast of Jonah:

The fast of Jonah was introduced by Pope Abram the Syrian who himself introduced the three day fast of the moving of the Mokattam mountain. For being Syrian himself, he kept up the fast of Jonah which the Syrian church observed. Now when he was ordained a Patriarch of the Coptic church, he observed it in its time, and the people followed suit and kept this custom till this day. (41)

So then, if were the up to the Pope's choice to append this three day fast of the miracle, he would have added to the fast of Jonah, especially that the two fasts share a common nature, namely were fasts in times of distress.

For the fast of Jonah was observed because of the distress that the people of Nineveh had to go through, for which they implored the tender mercies of God, and the fast of the moving of the Mokattam mountain was because of the distress that came over the people of Egypt, for which they implored the tender mercies of God.

Furthermore, it is quite a small number of days if one adds three to three, which totals six days, while the addition of three to forty is quite the opposite. For 43 days are not a short period of time at all.

2) The addition to the fast of the Virgin Mary:

If it were up to the church to add the three day fast of the miracle to any other fast, it would have been to add it to the fast of the Virgin Mary (42), since it was the Virgin herself that appeared to the Patriarch and guided him to Saint Samaan the Tanner. So it would have rather added these three days to her fast to glorify her and in remembrance of her intercession.

But since these three days were added to neither of these two fasts, which otherwise deserve that this fast be added to them, then there remains the question: why were these three days appended to the Christmas fast?

In attempt to answer this question, we say that the Patriarch Abram the Syrian seems, on historical accounts, to have been quite minute as to keeping the dates of the fasts on their occasions, for history says:

> When the date of Nineveh's fast had fully come, he fasted it and his children followed suit, and therefore the Coptic church kept this custom till this day. (43)

So it is most probable, that the three day fast regarding the moving of the Mokattam mountain was fasted by the people just before the Christmas fast, and after the same fashion which our church kept till this day because that is when it actually happened.

The Christmas fast used to begin on November 28. each year and last till Christmas (January 7), which makes 40 days in all. But when the fast of the moving of the Mokattam was added to it, the sum total became 43 days and people began to observe it starting from November 25 every year. And since the miracle took place on the third day of the fast, then it took place on November 27.

71

So according to this research, it is true, the date of the miracle would be Hatur 18. 695 AM , namely November 27. 979 AD.

3) Celebrating the memory of this miracle:

At any rate, whether this assumption is correct or not, it is still fitting to celebrate the memory of this miracle during the first three days of the Christmas fast, namely from November 25. till November 27. every year, simply because they are the days that were appended to the Christmas fast in remembrance of this great miracle of moving the Mokattam mountain. For this reason, these three days in particular should be a period of spiritual revival, daily meetings, and divine masses for the memory of this supernatural wonder, for the victories of faith, and for the church's triumph over all the powers of evil, and over every weapon that formed against it, according to the sure and faithful divine promises.

"And I tell you that you are Peter, and on this rock I will build my church, and the gates of Hades will not overcome it." (Mt 16:18)

"No weapon forged against you will prevail, and you will refute every tongue that will accuse you." (Is 54:17)

My great God, I thank You because that which is impossible with men is possible with You. However great the mountain may be, Your power is much greater. My Lord, grant my complete faith and confidence in Your hand which raises mountains. Allow me, Lord, to come to You, imploring, "Lord, I believe. help my lack of faith." Let me place my small unable hand into Your big able hand that moves the mountains of weakness and doubt from my heart. And help me continue being confident in You, trusting You, proud of You. Amen.

CHAPTER 4

THE BUILDING OF ST. SAMAAN CHURCH IN MOKATTAM MOUNTAIN

1) The trash collectors in Mokattam.
2) A trash collector calls a minister.
3) The confirmation of God of the calling
4) Fleeing like Jonah.
5) The miracle of a whirlwind that carried a heavenly message.
6) Choosing the site of the church.
7) Building a church of tin.
8) Replacing tin with bricks.
9) The present church building.
10) The miracle of the water needed for building.
11) The miracle of healing a smashed head.
12) His Holiness the Pope visits the church.

*"He raises the poor from the dust and lifts the
needy from the ash heap; he seats them with
princes, with the princes of their people. "
(Ps 113:8)*

1) THE TRASH COLLECTORS LIVE ON A HILL ON THE MOKATTAM.

At the end of 1969 his excellency the governor of Cairo issued a decree to the end of removing all the trash collectors of Cairo to one of the hills of the Mokattam to live there.   So they built themselves primitive houses, simply huts of tin that are called in their vernacular *"Zaraayib"* (namely pigsties). They were thus named after the place where donkeys and pigs live, and all the other livestock they reared up; such as goats and cattle.

The number of the trash collectors that live in that area reached about 15,000 according to the research of the International Bank which was carried out in July, 1987. But, by the grace of God, this number has doubled now.

Every person had a primitive trash cart that looked like a wooden box carried on two wheels and pulled by two donkeys, or more, because of the difficult hill upto the mountain which was not paved in the past.

These trash collectors collect trash from the houses of most sectors of Cairo, and upon returning to their huts, they sort out the trash and classify it. They pick out from the trash all that is fitting for pigs and cattle to eat, as for the paper, glass, plastic, cloth and stuff like that, they are resold to specialized tradesmen, after they are sorted out, and the trash collectors live on what they get from selling them.

2) A TRASH COLLECTOR CALLS A MINISTER.

A trash collector named *Qiddees Ageeb Abd Al-Maseeh* used to collect trash from the area of Shubra, and used to meet a certain minister, who told him about the life with God and enjoying His love and grace through repen- tance.

Qiddees invited this minister to visit the Zabbaleen (the Garbage City) area in the Mokattam, and he repeated this invitation for the period of two years, from 1972-1974. But the minister would not respond.

3) GOD CONFIRMS THE CALLING

On the morning of the first Friday in February 1974, this trash collector met the same minister, and urged him to visit the area. The minister, then, heard the voice of God inside him confirming that this calling was from Him.

The minister asked the trash collector how he could reach this area, and he told him to take a bus to the foot of the Mokattam mountain and to wait for the bus line that would take him to the Zaraayib area.

4) FLEEING LIKE JONAH.

The minister went to the bus stop and instead of taking the bus going to the Mokattam he thought better of it and tried to escape like Jona, he got on the bus going to the opposite direction: to Matariya!

But the divine inner voice repeated its demand to get off this bus and go to the Zaraayib, as he was told before. He obeyed and, when he reached the terminal, he found Qiddees waiting for him. He went up the hill, on which the Zaraayib were erected.

At the entrance of this area, while the trash carts were tremendously active, carts going up and others coming down, a great number of men, boys, and girls; some of them were driving the carts while others helped push the donkey uphill against the difficulty of the road, the minister stood overwhelmed by a strange feeling that God wanted to do something in this area! But what is it that God wanted in particular? He did not know. Therefore, he asked the trash collector to take him to a quiet place to pray.

He took him to the highest place of this area, and there he found a big gap under a huge rock. It was a strange cave (which is now in the monastery of Saint Samaan the Tanner). But the minister found it a suitable place for prayer, and he kept on praying in it every Sunday for three weeks, without ever talking to any of the trash collectors that filled the place and spread themselves over that part of the mountain like locusts.

He would ask God in his prayers, "Lord, what do you want me to do?" (Acts 9:6). In the third week, a strange thing happened...

5) THE MIRACLE OF A WHIRLWIND THAT CARRIED A HEAVENLY MESSAGE.

In the third week, the minister went up to the cave, taking along two other persons. While they were praying, a whirlwind arose causing all the paper in the area and the trash to be strewn everywhere. When the whirlwind subsided, a small piece of paper fell before the three, one of them took it and gave to the minister to read its content. To their surprise, it was a page from Acts 18 ! The minister's eyes fell upon the verses, which read: "The Lord spoke to Paul in a vision: *"Do not be afraid; keep on speaking, do not be silent. For I am with you, and no-one is going to attack and harm you, because I have many people in this city."* (Acts 18:9,10)

The minister considered this to be God's voice speaking to him, or as H. H. Pope Shenouda III has commented, "It was not a mere piece of paper, but a heavenly edict." From that time on, the minister began to evangelize to this area seriously.

6) CHOOSING THE SITE OF THE CHURCH

The minister, together with another one, started to look for a place to minister, even to Sunday School kids. They stood in a place at the edge of the area, and the first minister remembered what he had heard from his Father Confessor when the latter preached, reiterating the saying in Joshua 1:3, *"I will give you every place where you set your foot."*

In simplicity of faith, he began to set his foot on the place where he was standing without telling his colleague anything about what was going on inside him, especially that he found him moving in the opposite direction. Then they met while turning around the place in opposite direction. the minister asked his colleague what he was doing, for which he gave an answer that astonished the other minister. he said, "Isn't it written in Joshua that "I will give you every place where you set your foot"?!!

The minister was assured that this was the place that God appointed for them as a site of a church in the Mokattam, which has now come true.

7) BUILDING A CHURCH OF TIN.

After choosing the place, work was begun on a church made of tin, with a roof made of reeds, just like the roofs of the rest of the area, which brought back memories of the manger in Bethlehem.

The ministry to the Sunday School kids started, and on the first day eleven kids attended. After that a general meeting for men and women was started. The attendance on the first day, which was April 13. 1974, wsa nine people.

Even though this was not an encouraging beginning, yet it pushed these two ministers to pray all the more, and visit the huts one by one, speaking with everyone about the love of the Lord Jesus Christ and about the way to repentance.

After nearly five months, the place could no longer contain all who came. The Lord had blessed the work through the prayers of the Saint of this mountain, Samaan the Tanner.

8) REPLACING THE TIN WITH BRICKS

When the place became too small, the two ministers, together with a third one, whom the Lord had added to them, were obliged to enlargen the place by the help of the Lord. So they replaced the tin with bricks and reinforced concrete. But the roof was made of canvas, which made the place look like the Tabernacle on top of the holy mountain!

9) THE PRESENT CHURCH BUILDING.

After the church was completely built with bricks, the minister went, along with his Father Cofessor, to H. H. Pope Shenouda III and told him everything that had been done. He greatly rejoiced and encouraged his children the ministers and gave a certain sum of money to build a roof of concrete.

However, something happened that obliged the ministers to tear down that building and erect the present church, which was the third attempt to build a place suitable for the holiness of God.

It so happened the attendance multiplied in an amazing way, and multitudes came to the church, which made the place too small for them all. This compelled the minister to turn to a helpful architect, who planned a wonderful design for the church. Thus the building started till it became the lofty one we see now covering an area of about 1000 sq.m.

Many miracles took place to bring this gorgeous building to its present state.

10) THE MIRACLE OF PROVIDING WATER FOR THE BUILDINGS.

After buying the building materials, namely gravel, cement, steel, and bricks, work could still not begin due to the need for water. This was especially so in that desert area whose inhabitants could not find water for their necessary needs at that time.

Fervent prayers were lifted up and the miracle took place. One evening when the minister was returning, he found at the edge of the paved road leading up to the Mokattam City a tractor pulling a huge water container. He asked the driver to provide him with the water necessary for the building of the church. The man agreed on the spot with no hesitation. This was the assistance of heaven!

11) THE MIRACLE OF HEALING A SMASHED HEAD.

One of the miracles that the Lord performed during the building of the church was the following. On Monday January 19. 1977, after the tractor had unloaded its cargo of water, and while trying to back up, there was a child standing behind it named *Adham Kamel Abd Al-Maseeh,* aged 6 years, who fell under the huge container's wheels. His head was bashed in under them, and he was hurried to the hospital in a coma. The evening meeting was turned into a prayer meeting for Adham, so that the Lord might perform a miracle and heal him.

On the fourth day, the two ministers went to visit the child in the hospital and found him lying still on the bed and his head was smashed, while blood was gushing out of his nose, ears, and mouth.

The two minister stood by the bed, asking the Lord to perform a miracle to this child, and create him a new head, through the intercession of Saint Samaan the Tanner the patron Saint of this church.

After seven days, the Lord glorified Himself and answered the prayer. Adham returned home in good health; he remains a witness to our living God who can do everything and there is nothing too difficult for Him.

12) H. H. THE POPE VISITS THE CHURCH.

June 18, 1977. was an unforgettable day in the history of the church, for on that day H. H. Pope Shenouda III visited the church. His visits to the church were repeated every year on the feast of Saint Samaan the Tanner from 1978 till 1980.

The church of Saint Samaan the Tanner receives a special attention from His Holiness.

My great God, I thank You because you are the same yesterday, today and

87

for ever. You are with us always and unto the end of the age. You build Your church and the gates of hell shall not prevail against it. You lift it up for ever, meeting all its needs according to Your riches in glory. I pray for this vineyard, which Your right hand has planted: Make it good and establish it, so that it might be fruitful and that its fruit might continue in it. Through the prayers of our father Saints, and our father, the man of faith, Samaan the Tanner, do we pray. Amen.

CHAPTER 5

THE DISCOVERY OF THE BODY OF THE GREAT SAINT OF FAITH SAMAAN THE TANNER

1) An erroneous belief.
2) How the body of Saint Samaan the Tanner was discovered.

1) AN ERRONEOUS BELIEF.

Down the years, an untrue account of the way Saint Samaan the Tanner died stuck in the minds of many members of the Church.

In short, this account holds that **the Saint threw himself under the Mokattam mountain, or into it, so that the present people should not honor him for the miracle of moving the mountain.**

Does this account agree with the church history and ordinance that were handed down to us down the generations?

The truth is that this account contradicts the church completely. Our proof consists in the following:

First: The description of the chroniclers of the miracle:

The first one to write down the miracle of moving the Mokattam Mountain was Anba Saweeris Ibn Al-Muqaffaa, the bishop of Ashmunin. That bishop was the Saint who accompanied Pope Abram in his debate with

Moses the Jew in the presence of the caliph Al-Mu'iz Li Din Illah Al-Fatimi, as we have mentioned above. He has recorded the biography of Anba Abram in his book *THE HISTORY OF THE PATRIARCHS*.

This honorable scholar has, therefore, witnessed the miracle in all its stages, and written it down most clearly in his writing of the biography of Pope Anba Abram Ibn Zaraa.

All the chroniclers and composers of church songs have adopted Anba Saweeris' description of the miracle. None of them mentioned anything contradictory to his description, for he was an eye-witness and a source for all of them as far as the miracle is concerned.

In his description of the miracle:

1) He did not mention anything at all that agrees whatsoever with this strange account that Saint Samaan threw himself under the mountain.

2) He mentioned that Saint Samaan made a condition, in his first meeting with Pope Abram, that no one should know about him until he was translated from this world, which the Pope promised to do;

The man, Saint Samaan, stood during the moving of the Mountain, and no-one of the multitude knew him, but for the Patriarch.

In the thirteenth century AD, bishop Usab, the bishop of Fuwwa, said while describing the first meeting between the Pope and Saint Samaan, that Saint Samaan said to the Pope:

Now I ask you not to divulge my secret, and not to tell it to anyone. Let me be behind you. When you worship, let me worship with you, and when you draw the sign of the cross, let me do the same with you; without letting anybody know.

Then why could the Saint throw himself under the mountain so that the people might not honor him, while no one knew him to start with?

Second: The description of the chroniclers of the disappearance of Saint Samaan the Tanner after the performance of the miracle:

Both Anba Saweeris and Anba Usab described how Saint Samaan disappeared directly after the miracle of moving the mountain.

In his book *THE HISTORY OF THE PATRIARCHS* he says:

When they calmed down, the Patriarch turned around seeking the holy man Samaan the Tanner, but did not find him.

In a manuscript in the Syrian monastery, Anba Usab says:

Then the Patriarch turned around looking for the Tanner [Saint Samaan] but found him not.

From what was mentioned above in chapter 3 we know that Saint Samaan was standing directly behind Anba Abram, for the Pope turned around and looked behind him. Now, if Saint Samaan threw himself under the mountain, the Pope would have seen him. Also the fact that he needed to look behind him searching for him, tells us either of these two things:

1) Either Saint Samaan departed in silence and great humility as soon as the miracle was performed, as his Lord Jesus Christ of whom the Bible says, **"Jesus, knowing that they intended to come and make him**

king by force, withdrew again to a mountain by himself." (Jn 6:15)

2) Or maybe the chroniclers wanted to point to some sort of miraculous disappearance, such as the transference of some of the Anchorite Saints, just as the Bible narrates the transference of apostle Philip (Acts 8:39) "The Spirit of the Lord suddenly took Philip away, and the eunuch did not see him again."

2) HOW THE BODY OF SAINT SAMAAN THE TANNER WAS DISCOVERED.

First: Locating the burial-place of Saint Samaan the Tanner:

In the beginning of 1989, Gog laid it on the heart of a certain minister to look for the remains of the Saints and the martyrs buried in Old Cairo. So he looked also for the burial-place of Saint Samaan the Tanner. As a result of the guidance of Providence, he found out that that great Saint of faith Samaan the Tanner was buried in a cemetery called Al-Habash in Old Cairo.

Some of the most important references this minister depended on in his search were:

1) The Synaxarion (martyrologium) of Abib 19. on the death of Anba Yo`annas the tenth Pope. (85)

> *On the same day as this in 1085 AM in July 13. 1369, the tenth Pope Yo`annas rested in peace and was buried next to Samaan the Tanner.*

2) In THE HISTORY OF THE PATRIARCHS by Anba Usab, we read in the biography of Pope Yo`annas X:

> *He died and was buried in Al-Habash next to the Tanner.*

3) The Synaxarion of Bashans 3. on the death of Pope Anba Ghubrial IV (86):

> *On the same day as this in 1094 AM in April 13. 1378, Pope Ghubrial rested in peace and was buried in Al-Habash next to the Tanner.*

4) In THE HISTORY OF THE PATRIARCHS by Anba Usab, in the biography Pope Ghubrial IV, we read:

He rested in peace and was buried in Al-Habash next to the tanner.

The important result of this research is that:

1) **Saint Samaan the Tanner was buried in Old Cairo.**

2) **Saint Samaan the Tanner was buried in Al-Habash cemetery in Old Cairo.**

3) **Saint Samaan the Tanner was buried next to two Patriarchs.**

The search was conducted in the period from 1989 to 1991.

Second: The appearance of the body of Saint Samaan the Tanner.

1991 was a very blessed year, for Providence had predestined it that the restoration of the ancient church of Saint Mary in Babylon El-Darag in Old Cairo should start that year. On Sunday August 4. 1991, during the restoration and excavating of the eastern wall of the church from the outside, exactly as deep as 3 meters from the surface of the club adjacent to the wall, and as deep as 1 meter from the surface of the church, a skeleton of a buried person was found adjacent to the southern wall of the church from outside. When this skeleton appeared, divine awe and spiritual gladness came over all those present, and we felt that the atmosphere was filled with invisible spiritual hosts hovering over the place.

This skeleton belongs to a person who died in his late forties, or in his early fifties. He is short of stature, small in size, of brilliant and beautiful features. The miraculous wonder is that the hair of his head remained intact and did not disintegrate because of the high humidity of the place. This indicated that this person had a bald head in the front, but had very thick hair in the back of his head that reached down to the back of his neck.

The icon of Anba Abram with Saint Samaan the Tanner, which is kept in the Suspended church of Saint Mary, Old Cairo, confirms several features of Saint Samaan the Tanner, which in turn are identical with the features of the discovered skeleton. These characteristics consist in his short stature, peculiar kind of hair, and the anatomical arrangement of his skeleton.

There was also found beside the excavation, on another side outside the church of the Saints

Abakeer and Yohanna in the same place, a clay pot that is more than a thousand years old, which indicates that this body belongs to Saint Samaan the Tanner as Saint Mary told Pope Abram, before the miracle was performed. This pot is now in the compartment belonging to Saint Samaan in his church in Mokattam, Cairo.

Up till that moment, it was not known for sure who this body belonged to, or if it belonged to Saint Samaan.

What was left undone was to connect this burial-place and the so-called Al-Habash cemetery, so that it would be made sure that this body belonged to Saint Samaan the Tanner.

In a meeting between H. H. the honorable reverent Anba Mattaos, the general bishop of Old Cairo at the time and the abbot of the Syrian monastery now, and the minister, who carried out this search on the where-abouts of Saint Samaan's body, H. H. Anba Mattaos asked him to proceed with his search. The minister went out after that.

Only one hour after this meeting, the Lord sent an important reference book to this minister which located the cemetery called Al-Habash. The following is a quotation from it:

Al-Habash cemetery in Old Cairo is the same area in which the excavation in the church of Saint Mary in Babylon El-Darag is being carried out. in this place the remains of more than 13 Saints were uncovered, among whom were Patriarchs, a tube containing the head of a martyr child and the body of Saint Samaan the Tanner. At that time we were wondering why the Patriarchs were buried outside the church.

Saint Samaan continued to appear to many of the Fathers of the church, confirming that this body belonged to him personally. The fathers were amazed of the way all the features in the icon in the Suspended church of Saint Mary fit him.

Furthermore, a copy of the research was handed to H. H. Pope Shenouda III which contained a detailed report on how the owner of this body was discovered and identified, and on the circumstances, the visions and the appearances which accompanied this. H. H. studied the research and the report with utter thoroughness, after which H. H. declared the dependability of this research and his own belief in the fact that this was truly the body of Saint Samaan the Tanner the mover of the

Mokattam mountain. He declared this during his holiness' meeting with the father priests in Cairo on Tuesday July 1992, and H. H. Anba Mattaos was also present. It was such a great day that the Lord has made, in which the heavenly beings and the earthly rejoiced and were glad.

Then H. H. the Pope ordered that the body should be divided between three churches only, which were:

1) The church of Saint Mary in Babylon El-Darag.

2) The Suspended church of Saint Mary.

3) The church of Saint Samaan the Tanner in the Mokattam.

On Thursday July 9, 1992 H. H. Anba Mattaos took it upon himself to deposit part of the body of Saint Samaan the Tanner in a tube in the church of Saint Mary in Babylon El-Darag. He also wrote the document that goes with it, and these are now next to the compartment of Saint Samaan the Tanner in the Mokattam, Cairo.

On Saturday July 11, 1992 and in an awesome spiritual procession, the remains of Saint Samaan the Tanner were removed to his church in Mokattam. It was a historic day on which heaven rejoiced, and the believers were glad that the man of faith and the example of holiness and temperance had come to them.

My God and Lord Jesus Christ, how I do thank You for this blessed life of whom You spoke to them. Now I feel how weak I am against this strength of faith, and how sinful I am against this life of temperance and holiness which Saint Samaan the Tanner lived.

I put the lack of my faith and my many sins, or rather my whole being, at Your feet. My Lord, re-form me afresh as a vessel of honor suitable for the use of the Master, so that I may be ready for every good work, through the blessing of my Fathers the apostles, the Saints, the confessors, and the martyrs, whose good works pleased You, and *through the blessing of the patron Saint of this church Samaan the Tanner, the blessing and prayers of our blessed and honorable father Pope Shenouda III, together with the bishops and archbishops. Amen.*

Footnotes

1) Iris El-Masri, *The Story of the Coptic Church*, part 3, p. 15.

2) Pastor Manassah Yohanna, *The History of the Coptic Church*, p. 436.

3) Dr. Hasan Al-Basha, *Cairo*. p. 9.

4) Anba Isodorus, *Al-khareeda Al-nafeesa fi Tareekh Al-kaneesa*, p. 88.

5) Iris El-Masri, *The Story of the Coptic Church*, part 3, p. 15.

6) A manuscript in the Anba Antonios monastery.

7) Iris El-Masri, *The Story of the Coptic Church*, part 3, p. 26.

8) A manuscript in the Anba Antonios monastery.

9) Ibid.

10) Iris El-Masri, *The Story of the Coptic Church*, part 3, p. 27.

11) Pastor Manassah Yohanna, *The History of the Coptic church*, p. 431.

12) Iris El-Masri, *The Story of the Coptic Church*, part 3, p. 27.

13) A manuscript in the Anba Antonios
monastery.

14) Iris El-Masri, *The Story of the Coptic
Church*, part 3, p. 27.

15) A manuscript in the Anba Antonios
monastery.

16) Ibid.

17) Ibid.

18) Ibid.

19) Ibid.

20) Iris El-Masri, *The Story of the Coptic
Church*, part 3, p. 28.

21) A manuscript in the Antonios monastery.

22) Iris El-Masri, *The Story of the Coptic
Church*, part 3, p. 27.

23) Ibid., p. 28.

24) ***Birkit El-phil:*** was cultivated piece of
land where the Mokattam mountain
was before it was removed. Now it is
known by Al-Hilmiya Al-Gadeeda.
(Adapted from *AL-NUGUUM AL-
ZAAHIRA FI MULUUK MASR WAL
QAHIRA, by Al-Atabky*, part 3, p.
365,366).

25) Pastor Manassah Yohanna, *The History
of the Coptic Church*, p. 430.

26) Iris El-Masri, *The Story of the Coptic Church*, part 3, p. 27.

27) Ibid.

28) A manuscript in the Anba Antonios monastery.

29) *Al-mu'gam Al-waseet.*

30) Iris El-Masri, *The Story of the Coptic Church*, part 3, p. 34.

31) *Kitaab Al-fatimiyeen Fi Misr.*

32) Pastor Manassah Yohanna, *The History of the Coptic Church*, p. 432.

33) Dr. Ra`ouf Habib, *The Ancient Coptic Churches in Cairo*, p. 22.

34) A manuscript in the Anba Antonios monastery.

35) Pastor Manassah Yohanna, The History of the Coptic Church, p. 431.

36) Iris El-Masri, The Story of the Coptic Church, part 3, p. 28.

37) Dr. Ra`ouf Habib, The Ancient Coptic Churches in Cairo, p. 60.

38) Iris El-Masri, The Story of the Coptic Church, part 3, p. 26.

39) Pastor Manassah Yohanna, The History of the Coptic Church, p. 431.

40) Ibid., p. 432.

41) Ibid.
42) The fast of Saint Mary which lasts for 15 days, starting from the beginning of the month of Masra and ending on the fifteenth of the same month. The church celebrates on the 16. of Masra the ascension of the body of Saint Mary to heaven
43) Pastor Manassah Yohanna, The History of the Coptic Church, p. 432.

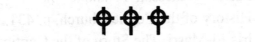

THE INDEX

❄❄❄

THE INDEX

⌘ ⌘ ⌘